W9-CNE-905

Rocks and Fossils

KINGFISHER
LONDON & NEW YORK

Copyright © Kingfisher 2011
Published in the United States by Kingfisher,
175 Fifth Ave., New York, NY 10010
Kingfisher is an imprint of Macmillan Children's Books, London.
All rights reserved.

Distributed in the U.S. by Macmillan, 175 Fifth Ave., New York, NY 10010

Library of Congress Cataloging-in-Publication data has been applied for.

ISBN: 978-0-7534-6606-3

First published as *Kingfisher Young Knowledge: Rocks and Fossils* in 2003
Additional material produced for Kingfisher by Discovery Books Ltd.

Kingfisher books are available for special promotions and premiums.
For details contact: Special Markets Department, Macmillan, 175 Fifth Ave., New York, NY 10010.

For more information, please visit www.kingfisherbooks.com

Printed in China
1 3 5 7 9 8 6 4 2
1TR/0511/WKT/UG/140MA

Note to readers: the website addresses listed in this book are correct at the time of going to print. However, due to the ever-changing nature of the Internet, website addresses and content can change. Websites can contain links that are unsuitable for children. The publisher cannot be held responsible for changes in website addresses or content or for information obtained through a third party. We strongly advise that Internet searches be supervised by an adult.

Acknowledgments
The publisher would like to thank the following for permission to reproduce their material. Every care has been taken to trace copyright holders. However, if there have been unintentional omissions or failure to trace copyright holders, we apologize and will, if informed, endeavor to make corrections in any future edition.
b = bottom, *c* = center, *l* = left, *t* = top, *r* = right

pages: *cover* Shutterstock Images; 1 Corbis; 2–3 Corbis; 4–5 Geoscience Features; 6–7 Corbis; 7*br* C. & H. S. Pellant; 8–9 Corbis; 9*tr* G. Brad Lewis/Science Photo Library; 10–11 (sky) Dynamic Graphic; 10*tr* C. & H. S. Pellant; 10*bl* Corbis; 11 Corbis; 12–13 Geoscience Features; 12*cl* C. & H. S. Pellant; 13*cl* C. & H. S. Pellant; 14–15 Corbis; 15*tl* C. & H. S. Pellant; 15*cr* Science Photo Library; 16*cl* C. & H. S. Pellant; 16–17 Corbis; 17*tl* Geoscience Features; 18–19 Corbis; 19*tl* Frank Lane Picture Library; 19*cr* Frank Lane Picture Library; 20–21 (sky) Dynamic Graphic; 20–21 (rock) Science Photo Library; 21*tr* Corbis; 21*br* Corbis; 22–23 Corbis; 22*tl* Science Photo Library; 23*tr* Corbis; 24–25 Science Photo Library; 25*tl* Digital Science; 25*br* Corbis; 26–27 Corbis; 26*bl* Corbis; 27*l* Corbis; 28–29 Corbis; 28*bl* David M. Dennis/Oxford Scientific Films; 29*tl* Corbis; 30–31 Corbis; 30*b* Science Photo Library; 31*c* Corbis; 32–33 Corbis; 32*bl* Corbis; 33*b* Corbis; 34–35 Corbis; 34*br* Ardea; 35*tl* Science Photo Library; 35*r* Corbis; 36–37 Michael Fogden/Oxford Scientific Films; 37*t* Science Photo Library; 37*cr* Geoscience Features; 38–39 Corbis; 39*tr* Corbis; 39*cl* Science Photo Library; 40–41 David M. Dennis/Oxford Scientific Films; 40*b* Science Photo Library; 41*cr* Science Photo Library; 42–43 Geoscience Features; 42*bl* Corbis; 43*tr* Corbis; 45*tr* Geoscience Features; 46*tr* Corbis; 48 iStockphoto/Josef Friedhuber; 49*t* Shutterstock Images/markrhiggins; 49*b* Shutterstock Images/alexia; 52*t* Shutterstock Images/dinadesign; 52*b* Wikimedia/Meckimac; 53*t* Shutterstock Images/Ziga Camernik; 53*b* iStockphoto/Kun Jiang; 56 Shutterstock Images/Roger De Marfa

Commissioned photography on pages 44–45 by Geoff Dann; 46–47 by Andy Crawford
Thank you to models Daniel Newton and Eleanor Davis

Rocks and Fossils

Chris Pellant

KINGFISHER
NEW YORK

Contents

What is a rock? 6

Rocks from heat 8

Rough and smooth 10

Secondhand rocks 12

Layer by layer 14

Rocks that change 16

Under pressure 18

Wear and tear 20

Rain, roots, and ice 22

Rocks from space 24

The uses of rocks 26

What is a fossil? 28

How fossils form 30

Ancient sea creatures 32

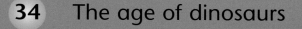

34 The age of dinosaurs

36 Fossil plants

38 Fossil fuels

40 Clues from fossils

42 How to find fossils

44 Project: Fun with fossils

46 Project: Rocks around you

48 Glossary

50 Parent and teacher notes

52 Did you know?

54 Rocks and fossils quiz

55 Find out more

56 Index

What is a rock?

Earth's crust is made of rocks. Some rocks are hard and solid, such as granite. Others are soft, such as sand. All rocks are made of minerals.

Craggy landscape

Here, in the Sierra Nevada, in the southwestern United States, weather has damaged a granite mountaintop and broken it into large, rounded boulders.

Grains of granite

Granite is made of different colored minerals. The pink mineral is called feldspar, the gray one is quartz, and the black one is mica.

8 Rocks from heat

Deep under Earth's crust, the rock is so hot that it is liquid. This molten rock is called magma. Sometimes the magma breaks through weak spots in the crust and reaches the surface. This is what happens when a volcano erupts.

Cooling lava

When the red-hot magma reaches the surface, it is called lava. Lava takes a long time to cool.

Igneous rocks

As the lava cools, it hardens and becomes rock. We call rocks that are made in this way, from heat, igneous rocks.

Rough and smooth

As molten rock cools, crystals are formed from the minerals. Large crystals grow if the rock cools slowly. Small crystals grow if the rock cools quickly.

Medium crystals

This microgranite rock has smaller crystals than granite because it cooled more quickly.

Lava columns

Basalt has tiny crystals and can have a smooth surface. It often cools into six-sided columns.

Cracks for climbing

Granite has large crystals. When granite magma cools, cracks form in the rock. Climbers grip the cracks as they climb.

Secondhand rocks

Sand, mud, and pebbles in a river or lake, or on the seabed, can be turned into rocks called sedimentary rocks. These can be told apart from other rocks because they have layers, or strata.

Shell rock
Limestone is often made of tiny shells. Curved snail shells can be seen in this rock.

sea cliff

Sandy cliffs

These cliffs in Dorset, U.K., are made of layers of sand that settled on the seabed millions of years ago. They have been tightly pressed together to form layers of rock.

Layer by layer

There are three different types of sedimentary rocks. One type is made of the remains of dead sea animals. Another is made of mud, sand, or pebbles. The third is made when water evaporates.

Tiny creatures
Limestone is made from the skeletons of millions of tiny sea creatures. It is worn away, or weathered, easily, often forming scenery like this.

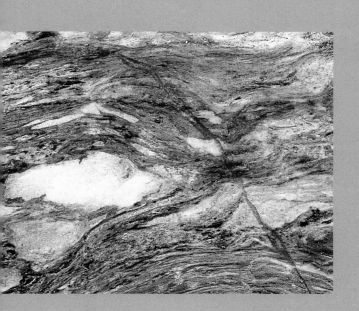

Rock gypsum

Seawater contains minerals. When it evaporates, minerals stay behind and form rocks, such as this gypsum.

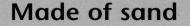

Made of sand

Sandstone is a very common rock. It often forms colorful layers, such as those you can see in this picture.

Rocks that change

Rocks change when they are heated deep underground—their crystals grow larger. Limestone, a sedimentary rock, turns into a metamorphic rock called marble. Layers in the rock disappear as it takes on a new form.

Fossil layers

Limestone is a rock that is formed in the sea and contains fossils. These fossils break down when the rock changes into marble.

Smooth marble

Marble has millions of pale crystals made of a mineral called calcite, stuck together tightly like a jigsaw puzzle.

Monumental rock

Marble is cut into many different shapes and used for decorations, sculptures, and gravestones.

Under **pressure**

As Earth's crust moves, any rocks deep down are twisted and squashed. Their shape is changed by pressure.

Twisted gneiss
Gneiss rock has twisted bands of dark and pale minerals. It used to be granite and is formed by the greatest pressure.

Slivers of slate

Slate is made when the pressure underground is not very strong. This rock breaks into thin slabs and can be used for roof tiles.

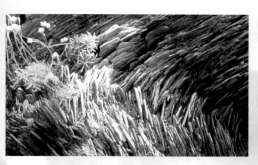

Silvery schist

Schist is formed in mountainous areas by medium pressure. Its silvery surface is covered with the mineral mica.

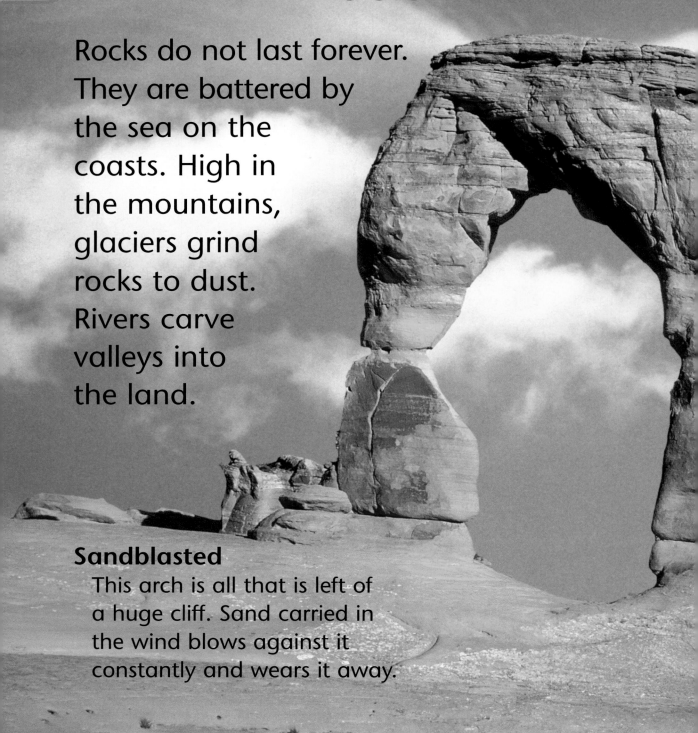

Wear and tear

Rocks do not last forever. They are battered by the sea on the coasts. High in the mountains, glaciers grind rocks to dust. Rivers carve valleys into the land.

Sandblasted
This arch is all that is left of a huge cliff. Sand carried in the wind blows against it constantly and wears it away.

Deep cuts

Rocks, sand, and pebbles carried in rivers pound against the riverbanks and can cut deep gorges into the land.

Wave power

Waves hurl rocks and stones at the cliffs, slowly breaking down the coastline.

Rain, roots, and ice

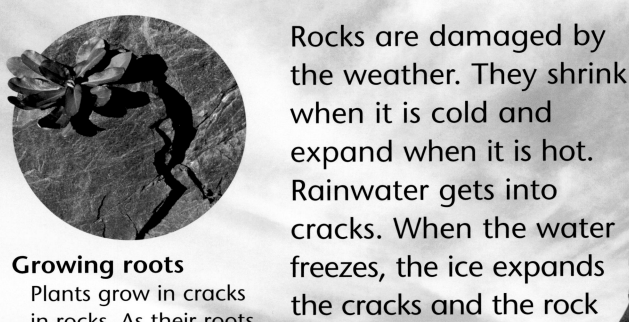

Growing roots

Plants grow in cracks in rocks. As their roots grow, they push the cracks farther apart.

Rocks are damaged by the weather. They shrink when it is cold and expand when it is hot. Rainwater gets into cracks. When the water freezes, the ice expands the cracks and the rock shatters.

Ice breaking

This mountain ridge shows how ice can break rocks apart to form jagged points.

Washed away

This rock is a strange shape because rainwater has weathered it over many years.

Rocks from space

In space, there are many rocks of different shapes and sizes. These are called meteors, and they are the rocks left over from when the planets formed. Sometimes, meteors crash down to Earth as meteorites.

Impact crater

This huge crater in Arizona was formed when a gigantic meteorite smashed into Earth. It is more than half a mile (1 kilometer) across—more than the length of 14 jumbo jets.

Explosive rock

When large meteorites hit the ground, they explode. The heat from the explosion melts the rocks around them, making glassy stones called tektites.

Hot metal

Most meteorites are made of metal, like this one. As they rush through the sky, they become extremely hot and can be seen as trails of light.

The uses of rocks

Rocks are used in thousands of ways. Without rocks, there would be no bricks, cement, glass, or coal. Most industry is based on the use of rocks.

Incredible clay
Clay is an important rock. As well as being used for pottery, it is used to make cement and even laundry detergent.

Angelic rock
Pale marble is a favorite rock for carving into statues, such as this angel.

Carved in stone
Many of the world's finest buildings are made from cut rock. Sedimentary rocks can be cut into neat blocks for building, and all rocks can be carved into delicate shapes.

What is a **fossil?**

Any trace of a plant or animal that lived in the past is a fossil, such as a shell preserved in rock layers for millions of years. The black outlines of delicate ferns and the massive footprints of dinosaurs are also fossils.

Trilobite
This creature lived in the sea hundreds of millions of years ago. Its modern relatives include insects, crabs, and spiders.

Big bones
These dinosaur bones were uncovered in Dinosaur National Monument in Colorado.

Uncovering the past
A fossil expert, or paleontologist, works very carefully to expose part of a huge dinosaur skeleton in Dinosaur National Monument.

How fossils form

Dead creatures and plants may be buried in sand or mud. This is when fossilization begins. The soft parts of the animal rot away, while the hard parts—its shell or bones— become fossilized.

Stuck fast, forever
This ant is caught in the sticky resin oozing from a tree. It will die there and may become a fossil.

Fossilized fly

Millions of years ago, this fly
became trapped in resin,
which hardened into amber,
fossilizing the fly.

Ammonites

Ammonites swam in the sea when
dinosaurs roamed the land. They are
close relatives of squids and octopuses.

ammonite

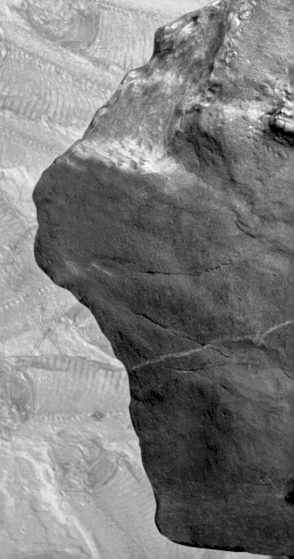

Ancient sea creatures

Fossils of dead sea creatures lie buried under the constant buildup of muddy and sandy layers on the seabed. Trilobites, corals, mollusks, and starfish are all common fossils from the ancient seas.

Tropical fossils

Corals build their homes out of limestone, often in tropical seas. Fossil corals tell geologists where these seas were long ago.

fossilized fish

Stone starfish

Even delicate animals such as this starfish can become fossilized. This fossil has formed in shale— a sedimentary rock formed on the seabed from packed mud.

The age of dinosaurs

Nobody has ever seen a dinosaur because they became extinct millions of years ago. We only know about dinosaurs from finding fossils of their bones, footprints, and eggs.

dinosaur fossil footprint

Buried in rock
This *Stegosaurus* fossil was found buried in Wyoming. It clearly shows the shape of the dinosaur.

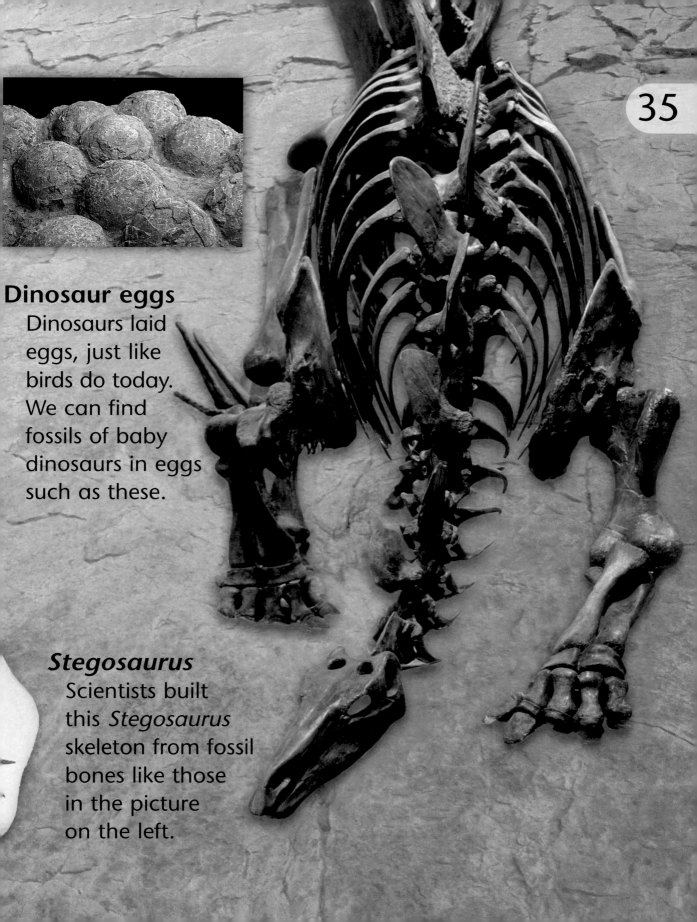

Dinosaur eggs

Dinosaurs laid eggs, just like birds do today. We can find fossils of baby dinosaurs in eggs such as these.

Stegosaurus

Scientists built this *Stegosaurus* skeleton from fossil bones like those in the picture on the left.

Fossil plants

Fossils of stems and tree trunks are common, especially in rocks that contain seams of coal. Among the seams, even fossils of delicate ferns may be found.

Stone trees

These trees were changed by fossilization—they are now made of a mineral called silica, instead of wood.

From old . . .

Delicate, beautiful fern leaves are fossilized as thin layers of carbon between the layers of rock.

. . . to modern

A modern-day fern is just like fossil ferns hundreds of millions of years old.

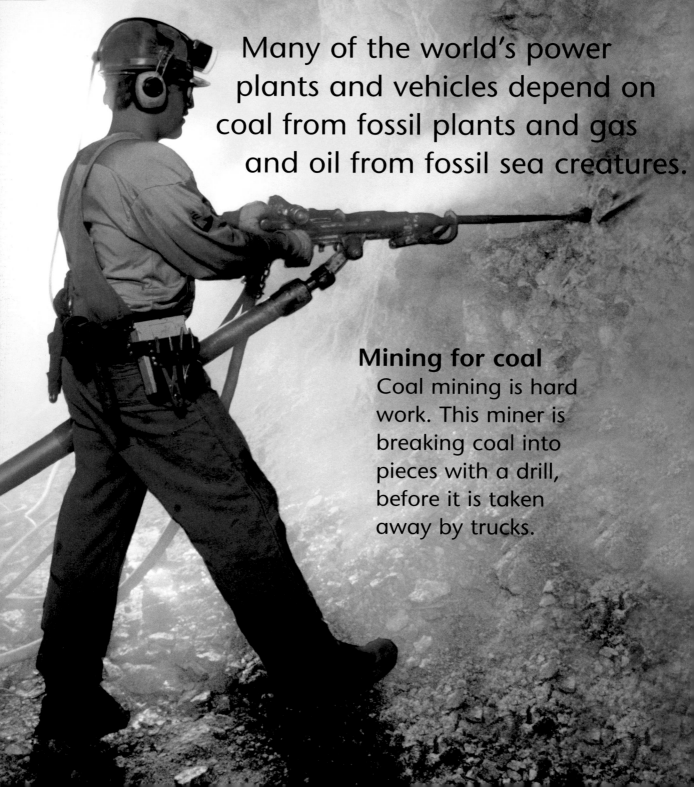

Fossil **fuels**

Many of the world's power plants and vehicles depend on coal from fossil plants and gas and oil from fossil sea creatures.

Mining for coal
Coal mining is hard work. This miner is breaking coal into pieces with a drill, before it is taken away by trucks.

Fossils for driving

Oil is a fossil fuel from which many products, including gasoline and diesel fuel, are made.

Poisonous fuel

Coal is a black, shiny rock. It has been used as a fuel for hundreds of years. However, when it is burned, poisonous smoke billows out and causes a lot of pollution.

Clues from fossils

Fossils tell us about life millions of years ago. Scientists can reconstruct the bodies of extinct creatures and study how animals and plants have evolved.

Alive and well

The coelacanth fish was known only as a fossil. Then, in 1938, living coelacanths were caught off the South African coast.

Historic footsteps

These footprints, made in soft mud more than three million years ago, show that our ancestors walked upright at that time.

archaeopteryx

Archaeopteryx

This is one of the most famous fossils. The skeleton looks like a small dinosaur, but there are impressions of feathers. Experts believe that modern-day birds are descended from dinosaurs.

How to find fossils

Fossils can be found close to cliffs or quarries or in other areas that have sedimentary rocks. However, these can be dangerous places, and you must never visit them without an adult.

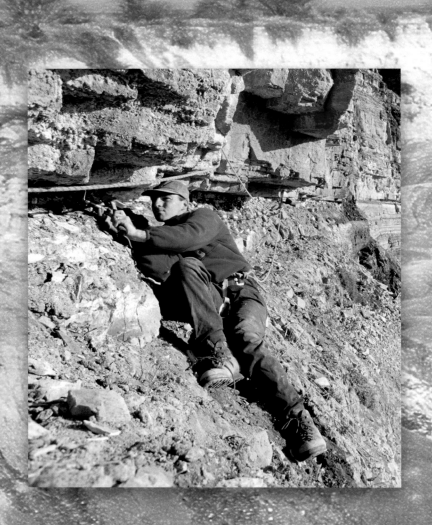

Cliffhanger
Paleontologists go to many different places to search for fossils, and it can be dangerous work. This fossil-hunter is carefully unearthing fossils on a steep slope.

Beach treasure

Fossils may fall
from cliffs and
land on the
beaches below.
Be careful around
cliffs and beware
of falling rocks.

Warning!

When rock is quarried, fossils
are often unearthed. Never
go to working quarries,
though—they can be
very dangerous.

Fun with fossils

You will need:
- 5 balls of colored dough
- Shells

Roll the dough into flat cakes. Sprinkle the first cake with shells. These will be your fossils.

Push the sides together to make an arch. This happens when rocks are squeezed together.

Making mountains
Layers of rock can be squashed together and forced up to make mountains. Any fossils in the layers then come to the surface.

Add two more layers of dough and shells. Then put two layers of dough on top. Do not put any shells in the top two layers.

Ask an adult to slice off the top. The first layers put down are now in the middle. They are the oldest layers and have the oldest fossils.

Amazing ammonites

Make your own fossil with modeling clay and plaster of Paris. Use a real fossil or a shell to make a cast.

You will need:
- Modeling clay
- Fossil or shell
- plaster of Paris
- Cup and spoon
- Paint
- Paintbrush

Roll some modeling clay into a ball. Press your fossil or shell, patterned side down, into the clay to make the cast.

Mix some plaster of Paris with water in a cup and carefully spoon or pour it into the cast. Leave it to set.

Once your fossil has set hard, carefully lift it from the cast. You may be able to use the cast again to make more fossils.

Your fossil is now ready to paint. Use any colors you want. Copy the colors of the shell or fossil or paint it in brighter colors.

Rocks around you

Rock collection

When you start rock collecting, label your rocks and record where you found them to organize your collection.

An egg carton is an ideal place for your collection. Use a different section for different types or colors of rocks. Paint your egg carton.

You will need:
- Egg carton
- Paint
- Paintbrush
- Cup for holding water
- Magnifying glass
- Sticky labels
- Notebook
- Pen

Examine the rock using a magnifying glass. You may be able to see the different colored minerals that form the rock.

Number all your rocks, starting from 1. Write the number of the rock on a sticky label and stick it onto the rock.

4

In your notebook, write the number, where and when you found the rock, and the rock type. If you do not know the type, leave a space to fill it in later.

5

Finally, once the paint on your egg carton has dried, put your rock into it, making sure that the label can be seen. Congratulations! You have begun your rock collection.

How are rocks used?
Rocks are used in many ways. Look around you at home and outside and draw the rocks that you see.

You will need:
- Notebook
- Pen

You may see rocks as part of a wall, sidewalk, or building. How many different uses for rocks can you find?

Glossary

carbon—a chemical found in coal, diamonds, and graphite

cement—a clay-limestone mixture that is used to make concrete

column—a tall, narrow pillar

crater—a hole in the ground made by a meteorite or a volcanic explosion

crust—Earth's outermost layer, some of which lies under oceans

crystal—a hard, glassy-looking object made of minerals

evaporate—when a liquid changes into a gas

evolved—to have changed gradually over time

expand—to get bigger

explode—to blow up, usually with a loud bang

extinct—when an animal or plant species has completely died out

fossil—the remains of a living thing from the past that is preserved in rock

fuel—a substance that can be burned to produce heat or power

glacier—a large, slow-moving mass of ice

gorge—a steep-sided valley carved into the land by a river

lava—molten rock on Earth's surface

magma—molten rock when it is underground

metamorphic—a change of form, usually by heat or pressure

mineral—one of the natural substances that make up different rocks

mollusk—a soft-bodied animal, such as a clam or a slug

mountainous—describes a high area of mountains

paleontologist—someone who studies fossils

pollution—chemicals, gases, and other materials that damage the environment

preserved—kept in good condition

pressure—when a weight is pressing down on something

quarry—a place from which stone is cut

reconstruct—rebuilding to show how something once looked

resin—the sticky sap that oozes from pine trees

seabed—the bottom of the sea

seam—a thin layer of a substance, such as coal

skeleton—the frame of bones inside an animal's body

strata—layers of rock

weathered—damaged or broken down by wind, water, or ice

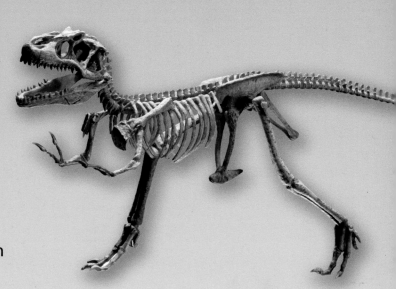

The content of this book will be useful to help teach and reinforce various elements of the science and language arts curricula in the elementary grades. It also provides opportunities for crosscurricular lessons in geography, art, and math.

Extension activities:

Writing
Pick up an ordinary rock. It has been around a very long time and been in many places, such as magma deep in Earth or perhaps part of a mountain ridge or carried along by a rushing river. Write an adventure story about where your rock might have come from and how it was moved from place to place.

Imagine that you've spent the day climbing along a rocky wall like the young woman in the photo on p. 11. Write a journal entry describing your experience. What was it like up there? What was the most exciting part? The scariest? The most fun?

Writing and oral language
Gather an assortment of rocks. Pick one and write a description of it. Put it back with the other rocks. Read what you wrote and see if others can tell which rock you are describing. If you are working with a group, have everyone do this together. Variation: Feel all the surfaces of your rock. Put it back in the pile. Close your eyes and see if you can find it using only your sense of touch. Talk about the clues that you are using.

Ask an adult to help you find reference books or websites about dinosaurs. Choose one that appeals to you and write a one-page report. Share your information with your family or class in a three-minute talk.

Science
The topic of rocks and fossils relates to the scientific themes of geology, Earth processes, fossils, and change over time/evolution.

Some specific links to science curriculum content include careers (pp. 29, 32, 35, 38, 40–42);

classification (pp. 8–9, 12–17); interaction with the environment (pp. 22–23, 38–39); materials (pp. 6–7, 10–19, 26–27, 38–39); properties of objects in the sky (pp. 24–25); scientific inquiry (pp. 29, 32–35, 40–43); and structure and function (pp. 32–35, 40–41).

Crosscurricular links
Geography
Many of the world's volcanoes are located in the Ring of Fire bordering the Pacific Ocean. See how many you can find on a map of this area.

Art
Use acrylic paints to decorate a rock. It could be a pretty design or something funny, like a creature. If you would like, make several and give them as gifts for people to use as paperweights.

Glue together several rocks (and perhaps some other natural materials) to make a sculpture.

Research and art
Using pictures of fossils from this book or other sources as a guide, make several drawings of different plant and animal fossils. For each one, write a paragraph of information about the fossil, including information such as what it is, where it was found, what it was like when it was alive, etc. Put your pages together to make a booklet.

Using the projects
Children can do these projects at home. Here are some ideas for extending them:

Page 44–45: Often scientists have only part of a fossil to work with and try to identify. Use modeling clay or dough to make a fossil-like impression of part of an everyday object. See if others can guess what it is. Try several different ones!

Page 46–47: How many different ways can you sort your rocks? Sort them by color, size, texture, luster (shininess), etc. Use various characteristics to divide them into groups. Arrange them to form real-world graphs and Venn diagrams.

Did you know?

- Diamonds are the hardest natural substance found on Earth.

- The most common rock on Earth is called basalt.

- There are more than 900 different types of igneous rocks.

- Almost 90 percent of Earth's upper crust is made out of igneous rock.

- The largest live volcano on Earth is Mauna Loa in Hawaii. It has been erupting on and off for at least 700,000 years!

- The largest ammonite fossils are often more than 20 inches (50 centimeters) in diameter.

- The Taj Mahal in India is made entirely out of marble.

- The Great Pyramid of Giza in Egypt is made entirely out of limestone.

- There are 1,500 active volcanoes around the world. At least 80 of these are found beneath the oceans.

- The longest dinosaur was called *Seismosaurus*. It measured more than 130 feet (40 meters) long—that is as long as three school buses.

- Globally, more electricity is produced by coal than by any other energy source.

- The largest meteorite crater on Earth is called the Vredefort crater. It is in South Africa and measures 186 miles (300 kilometers) in diameter.

- The oldest known fossil is 3.5 million years old.

- There are more than 3,000 different minerals in the world.

- The word *fossil* comes from the Latin word *fossilis*, which means "dug up."

Rocks and fossils quiz

The answers to these questions can all be found by looking back through the book. See how many you get right. You can check your answers on page 56.

1) What does igneous mean?
   A—made from water
   B—made from sand
   C—made from fire

2) What is someone who hunts for fossils called?
   A—biologist
   B—paleontologist
   C—zoologist

3) What is molten rock called?
   A—marble
   B—magma
   C—glacier

4) What sort of rock can fossils usually be found in?
   A—sedimentary
   B—igneous
   C—metamorphic

5) What are the layers that make up sedimentary rocks called?
   A—stacks
   B—lines
   C—strata

6) What is the mineral that makes up marble called?
   A—calcite
   B—brassite
   C—tantite

7) What is limestone made from?
   A—worms
   B—gravel
   C—skeletons of tiny sea creatures

8) How many types of sedimentary rocks are there?
   A—30
   B—3
   C—13

9) What are fossilized trees made out of?
   A—silica
   B—wood
   C—sand

10) Where is schist formed?
   A—mountainous areas
   B—lowland areas
   C—desert areas

11) Which of these rocks is formed when water evaporates?
   A—limestone
   B—gypsum
   C—marble

12) What are rocks that have fallen from space called?
   A—meteorites
   B—stalagmites
   C—kilobytes

Books to read

Fossils: History in the Rocks by Steven M. Hoffman, PowerKids Press, 2011

Fantastic Fossils (Rock on! A Look at Geology) by Christine Petersen, Abdo Publishing Company, 2010

Rocks and Minerals (Dorling Kindersley Handbooks) by Chris Pellant, Dorling Kindersley, 2010

Fossil Fuels (Future Energy) by Jim Ollhoff, Abdo Publishing Company, 2010

Rocks and Minerals: A Gem of a Book by Dan Green and Simon Basher, Kingfisher, 2009

Kingfisher Knowledge: Rocks and Fossils by Margaret Hynes, Kingfisher, 2008

Places to visit

Grand Canyon National Park, Arizona
www.nps.gov/grca/
For a truly memorable experience, visit the Grand Canyon, one of the seven natural wonders of the world. The canyon is more than 1 mile (1.6 kilometers) deep and exposes nearly two billion years of Earth's geological history.

American Museum of Natural History, New York City, New York
www.amnh.org/exhibitions/permanent/fossils/
The American Museum of Natural History is home to nearly one million fossil specimens. It also has an exhibit centered on a massive 34-ton (31-metric-tonne) meteorite fragment.

Reed Gold Mine, Midland, North Carolina
www.nchistoricsites.org/reed/reed.htm
Visit Reed Gold Mine, the site of the first documented gold find in the United States. Learn about the history of gold mining, the value of the gold recovered, and try panning for some gold yourself!

Websites

The Rock Cycle
www.cotf.edu/ete/modules/msese/earthsysflr/rock.html
Learn how the three types of rocks are made and how they are related to each other. Links lead to other sections on volcanoes, asteroids, and dinosaurs.

Fossils Rock!
www.fossils-facts-and-finds.com/
Everything you need to know about fossils. What they are, how they are formed, and where to go hunting for them. The site also has illustrations and photographs of many fossil examples.

Fossil Fuel Energy
http://tiki.oneworld.net/energy/energy3.html
What are fuels? How do you get energy from them? What is the big problem? Fossil fuels are covered here, together with renewable energy sources, and discussions on how you can save energy.

amber 31
ammonites 31, 52
archaeopteryx 41
basalt 10, 52
carving 17, 27
clay 26
cliffs 13, 21, 42–43
coal 36, 38, 39, 53
coelacanths 40
corals 32
crystals 10, 16
diamonds 52
dinosaurs 29, 34–35, 41, 53
erosion 20–21
fossil hunting 42–43
fossil plants 36–37, 38
fuels 38–39
gneiss 18
granite 7, 11, 18
igneous rocks 8, 9, 52
lava 8, 9
limestone 12, 14, 16, 53
magma 9
marble 16, 17, 27, 52
Mauna Loa 52
metamorphic rocks 16–17
meteorites 24–25, 53
minerals 6, 7, 10, 15, 53
paleontologists 29, 42

pyramids 53
sandstone 15
schist 19
sedimentary rocks 12–15, 27
shells 12, 28
slate 19
starfish 33
Taj Mahal 52
tektites 25
trilobites 28, 32
volcanoes 8, 52, 53
weathering 20–21, 22–23

Rocks and fossils
quiz answers

1) C	7) C
2) B	8) B
3) B	9) A
4) A	10) A
5) C	11) B
6) A	12) A